Microwave ovens do a lot more than heat up your coffee . . .

Do you take full advantage of your microwave oven's versatility?

Did you know that you can cook a wide range of foods, from Meat Loaf to Lamb Tossed with Spinach to Chinese Sweet and Sour Pork inside your microwave?

Well, you can . . .

And you can do it faster and easier than in your conventional oven!

A Treasury of Classic Microwave Recipes

Volume Three: Meat

by
Michelle A. Preston

Printed in the United States
All Rights Reserved

Copyright 1992

Table of Contents

Beef 7

Veal 73

Lamb 81

Pork and Ham 91

Variety Meats 125

BEEF

7

Beef with Ginger and Vegetables

1 medium can tomato soup
⅓ cup water
2 tablespoons soy sauce
2 teaspoons fresh ginger, grated
1 large clove garlic, minced
¾ pound beef flank steak, sliced thin
1 cup broccoli flowerets
1 large green pepper, cut into chunks

1) Mix together the soup, water, oil, soy sauce, ginger and garlic. Add the slices of meat, coating well. Cover and refrigerate for 2 hours.

2) Cover with vented plastic wrap and microwave on HIGH for 6 minutes or until the meat is no longer pink, stirring twice while cooking.

3) Add the broccoli flowerets and green pepper. Microwave, covered on HIGH for 5 minutes or until the vegetables are tender, stirring twice while cooking. Serve with or over rice, if desired.

California-Style
Meat Loaf

3 garlic cloves, minced
1 onion, chopped
1 celery stalk, chopped
2 tablespoons olive oil
1 teaspoon basil
1 teaspoon oregano
1 teaspoon thyme
1½ pounds lean ground beef
¾ pound bulk pork sausage
2 eggs, beaten
¼ cup dry bread crumbs
¼ cup chopped parsley
1 teaspoon salt
1 teaspoon pepper
4 ounces sun-dried tomatoes, diced

1) Place garlic, onion, celery and oil in a casserole dish. Microwave on HIGH for 5 minutes, stirring once while cooking. Mix in basil, oregano and thyme and set aside.

2) Combine beef, sausage, eggs, bread crumbs, parsley, salt and pepper. Add cooked vegetables and sun-dried tomatoes. Place in a loaf pan and cover with waxed paper.

3) Microwave on HIGH for 25 minutes. Let stand for 10 minutes before slicing.

Beef Stew

1 teaspoon butter
⅔ cup chopped onion
1 clove garlic, minced
1 pound chuck roast or beef for stew, cubed
1⅓ cup carrots, sliced thin
1 medium can gravy
¼ cup dry red wine
¼ cup tomato paste

1) Combine butter, onion, and garlic in a microwave-safe dish. Microwave, covered on HIGH for 2 minutes, stir, and cook for an additional 1 minute or until onion is tender.

2) Add meat, stirring to mix. Microwave, covered, on HIGH for 3 minutes, stir, and cook for an additional 2 minutes or until the meat is no longer pink.

3) Add carrots, gravy, red wine, and tomato paste, stirring to mix. Microwave, covered, on HIGH for 5 minutes or until stew begins to boil.

4) Stir, and microwave, covered, on MEDIUM for 30 minutes or until meat is tender, stirring twice during cooking.

5) Allow to stand, covered, for 5 minutes. Serve with or over noodles, if desired.

Roast Beef with Beer

4-pound beef top round roast, pierced with a fork
1 cup beer
2 cloves garlic, finely chopped
1 tablespoon vegetable oil
¼ teaspoon salt
¼ teaspoon pepper
2 teaspoons instant beef bouillon
¼ cup cold water
2 tablespoons all-purpose flour

1) Combine the beer, garlic, oil, salt and pepper. Place the beef into a bowl and pour the sauce over the beef. Cover and refrigerate for 1 hour, turning several times while marinating.

2) Sprinkle the roast with the beef bouillon and place the beef, fat side down, on a microwave rack in a baking dish. Reserve marinade.

3) Cover the roast with waxed paper and microwave on MEDIUM-LOW for 35 minutes. Turn the roast over, re-cover, and microwave on MEDIUM-LOW for 35 additional minutes. Remove from oven, cover with aluminum foil, and let stand for 15 minutes.

4) Place the drippings into a measuring cup. Skim off fat and add the reserved marinade and enough water to make 1 cup. Mix the ¼ cup of water and the flour together, and then stir into the marinade.

5) Microwave, uncovered, on HIGH for 3 minutes, stirring twice while cooking. Serve gravy on the side.

Beggar's Stew

1½ pounds ground beef
1 onion
3 carrots, scraped and chopped
1 large potato, peeled and chopped
¾ cup water
¾ cup catsup
1 tablespoon Worcestershire sauce

1) Combine beef and onions and microwave on HIGH for 6 minutes, stirring once while cooking. Drain.

2) Combine carrots, potato and 2 tablespoons of water in a bowl. Microwave, covered, on HIGH for 7 minutes. Drain.

3) Add in the beef, vegetables, catsup, remaining water, and Worcestershire sauce. Microwave, covered, on MEDIUM for 5 minutes.

Pizza-Topped Meat Loaf

2 pounds lean ground beef
½ cup oat bran
2 eggs
1 medium onion, chopped
1 large bottle pizza sauce
¾ teaspoon dry basil
¾ teaspoon dry oregano leaves
½ teaspoon pepper
½ teaspoon dry thyme leaves
¼ teaspoon garlic salt
1 small can sliced ripe olives, drained
6 large mushrooms, sliced thin
1 cup mozzarella cheese, shredded
½ cup Parmesan cheese, grated

1) Combine meat, oat bran, eggs, onion, ½ cup of the pizza sauce, basil, oregano, pepper, thyme, and garlic salt, mixing thoroughly. Place the mixture in a micro-wave-safe baking dish.

2) Microwave, uncovered, on HIGH for 12 minutes, giving the dish ½ turn every 4 minutes. Drain excess liquid from the dish, and spread the remaining pizza sauce over the top of the meat loaf. Sprinkle the olives and mushrooms over the top, followed by the two cheeses.

3) Microwave, uncovered, on HIGH, for 7 minutes, or until the meat loaf is no longer pink in center. Allow to stand, covered, for 5 minutes before serving.

Old-Fashioned Italian Meatballs

1 pound lean ground beef
1 egg
½ cup cracker crumbs
⅓ cup grated Parmesan cheese
1 tablespoon dried parsley
1 teaspoon garlic salt
16 ounces spaghetti sauce
1 tablespoon red wine

1) Combine all of the ingredients with the exception of the spaghetti sauce and the red wine, and form a dozen meatballs. Microwave, covered with waxed paper, on HIGH for 8 minutes. Drain.

2) Combine the spaghetti sauce and red wine and add the meatballs. Microwave, covered, on MEDIUM HIGH for 10 minutes. Allow to stand for 5 minutes before serving.

Sesame Beef

2 tablespoons sesame seeds, toasted
3 cloves garlic, finely minced
½ teaspoon minced fresh ginger
2 scallions, very finely minced
1 teaspoon soy sauce
1 teaspoon honey
1 teaspoon freshly squeezed lemon juice
1 pound lean top round, sliced against the grain into thin ribbons

1) Combine the sesame seeds, garlic, ginger, scallions, soy sauce, honey and lemon juice. Add beef, toss, and allow to marinate for 2 hours.

2) Place beef in a casserole, cover with vented plastic wrap and microwave on HIGH for 6 minutes, stirring twice while cooking. Allow to stand for 3 minutes before serving.

Traditional Roast Beef

1 5-pound rolled boneless beef rib roast
Brown Sauce (see below)

1) Coat the roast with sauce, and place on a microwave roasting rack.

2) Cover with waxed paper and microwave on HIGH for 30 minutes, rotating the dish once while cooking. Allow to stand for 15 minutes before carving.

Brown Sauce

½ cup molasses
⅓ cup corn syrup
1 tablespoon Worcestershire
1 teaspoon soy sauce

1) Combine the ingredients and microwave on HIGH for 2 minutes. Stir before pouring.

Meat Loaf with Carrots and Onions

1½ pounds ground chuck
1 onion, grated
2 carrots, grated
8 saltine crackers, finely crushed
1 egg
½ teaspoon salt
½ teaspoon pepper
1 tablespoon soy sauce
1 tablespoon catsup

1) Combine all of the ingredients with the exception of the soy sauce and catsup. Place in a baking dish and shape into a loaf.

2) Mix the soy sauce and catsup and brush onto the meat loaf. Cover with waxed paper, and microwave on HIGH for 18 minutes. Allow to stand, covered, for 5 minutes before slicing.

Flank Steak Stuffed with Vegetables

10 ounces frozen chopped spinach, thawed and drained
1 cup mushrooms, chopped
½ cup onion, chopped
1 clove garlic, minced
1 tablespoon olive oil
1 cup carrots, shredded
½ cup Swiss cheese, shredded
1 teaspoon dried basil leaves, crushed
¼ teaspoon pepper
1½ pounds beef flank steak, pounded to ¼-inch thickness
1 medium can cream of mushroom soup
2 tablespoons dry sherry

1) Combine spinach, mushrooms, onion, garlic, and oil in a microwave safe dish. Microwave, covered, on HIGH for 3 minutes. Stir, and cook for an additional 2 minutes or until the vegetables are tender.

2) Drain, and mix in the carrots, cheese, basil, and pepper. Spread the mixture over the steak, leaving a 1 inch rim around the edge. Roll the steak up from the long end, tucking the ends of the steak into the roll. Secure with wooden toothpicks, and place seam-side down in a large microwave-safe baking dish.

3) Stir soup until smooth and then mix in the sherry. Pour over the meat, and cover with vented plastic wrap.

4) Microwave on HIGH for 5 minutes. Rotate dish, and cook for an additional 5 minutes.

5) Spoon the pan juices over the meat. Microwave, covered, on MEDIUM for 7 minutes. Rotate the dish and cook on MEDIUM for an additional 7 minutes. Rotate the dish and cook on MEDIUM for 7 minutes more, or until the meat is tender. Allow to stand, covered, for 10 minutes before serving.

Ribs with Beer-Barbecue Sauce

4 beef short ribs
½ teaspoon freshly ground black pepper
8 tablespoons barbecue sauce
6 tablespoons beer

1) Sprinkle ribs with and pepper and place ribs, meaty side down, in a dish. Mix the barbecue sauce and beer and pour over ribs.

2) Cover with plastic wrap and microwave on HIGH for 25 minutes. Allow to stand for 1 minute before serving.

Meat Loaf with Wild Rice and Swiss Cheese

2 pounds lean ground beef
1 cup corn bread stuffing mix
8 ounces tomato sauce
½ cup chopped onion
¼ cup chopped celery
2 eggs
1 teaspoon thyme
½ teaspoon salt
½ teaspoon pepper
10½ ounces frozen wild rice
½ cup fresh mushrooms, sliced
½ cup Polish kielbasa sausage, diced
½ cup Swiss cheese, shredded
2 tablespoons parsley, minced

1) Combine beef, stuffing mix, tomato sauce, onion, celery, eggs, thyme, salt and pepper in a large bowl, and place in a bundt pan.

2) Pierce rice pouch with a fork and cook on HIGH for 4 minutes until defrosted. Place mushrooms, rice and sausage in the center of the meat loaf, then press the meat loaf over the filling, covering completely, and cover with waxed paper.

3) Microwave on HIGH for 15 minutes. Place on a serving platter and top with cheese and parsley.

4) Microwave on HIGH for 30 seconds, until cheese melts.

Corned Beef

3-pound corned beef boneless brisket
1 clove garlic, cut into 6 slivers
½ cup red wine
½ cup water

1) Cut 6 slits approximately ½-inch deep into the brisket and place a garlic sliver into each slit.

2) Place the brisket in a casserole dish and top with the wine and water. Microwave, covered, on MEDIUM-LOW for 2 hours, turning every 30 minutes.

Grandpa's Chili

1 pound ground beef
1 envelope onion soup mix
1 tablespoon chili powder
1 pound kidney beans
¼ cup water
1 large can tomatoes, with liquid,
quartered

1) Brown beef on HIGH for 6 minutes, stirring every 2 minutes. Drain grease.

2) Mix in the onion soup mix, chili powder, beans, water and tomatoes and liquid. Microwave on MEDIUM-HIGH for 10 minutes, stirring twice while cooking. Allow to stand for 5 minutes before serving.

Rump Roast

3 pound rolled rump roast
2 tablespoons dry onion soup mix
1 tablespoon water

1) Sprinkle roast with onion soup mix. Place roast in a casserole and add water.

2) Microwave, covered, on LOW for 60 minutes, turning 3 times while cooking. Allow to stand for 15 minutes before serving.

Garlic Beef

2 tablespoons freshly squeezed lemon juice
2 tablespoons soy sauce
2 cloves garlic, mashed to a paste
1 pound lean top round thinly sliced against the grain
4 coarsely chopped scallions
8 firm, flavorful tomato wedges
1 small bunch arugula leaves

1) Combine the lemon juice, soy sauce and garlic. Add the beef and allow to marinate for 3 hours.

2) Place the beef in a casserole, cover with vented plastic wrap, and microwave on HIGH for 5 minutes, stirring twice while cooking.

3) Allow to stand for 2 minutes, then toss with scallions, tomatoes and arugula leaves.

Rib Roast with Onion

1 5-pound rolled boneless rib roast
Water
1 package onion soup mix

1) Sprinkle the roast with water and completely cover with the onion soup mix. Place the roast on a microwave roasting rack with the fat side down.

2) Cover with waxed paper and microwave on HIGH for 30 minutes. Allow to stand for 15 minutes before carving.

My Mother's Meat Loaf

1 pound ground chuck
2 eggs, beaten
½ cup cracker crumbs
¼ cup catsup
2 tablespoons minced onion
¼ teaspoon salt
¼ teaspoon pepper
½ cup grated Cheddar cheese

1) Combine all of the ingredients with the exception of the cheese and place in a pie plate.

2) Cover with waxed paper and microwave on MEDIUM for 10 minutes, rotating the dish ½ turn after 5 minutes.

3) Remove drippings, top with cheese, and microwave on MEDIUM for 3 minutes. Allow to stand, covered, for 5 minutes before serving.

Japanese Steak

2 tablespoons soy sauce
1 tablespoon lemon juice
½ tablespoon brown sugar
½ teaspoon cornstarch
1 pound round steak, sliced across the grain into ¼-inch-thick strips
1 tablespoon sesame oil
1 garlic clove, minced
1 large onion, thinly sliced
1 teaspoon chopped fresh ginger
1 red pepper, cut into thin strips
1 green pepper, cut into thin strips

1) Combine the soy sauce, lemon juice, sugar, and cornstarch. Add the beef strips and marinate for 20 minutes at room temperature.

2) Combine the oil, garlic, onion, and ginger in a pie plate and microwave on HIGH for 3 minutes.

3) Place the onion in the center of the dish, and place the meat around the outer edge of the dish, reserving the marinade. Microwave, covered, on HIGH for 3 minutes. Stir the onion and the meat together.

4) Add the reserved marinade and the pepper strips. Microwave, covered, on HIGH for 3 minutes. Serve over rice.

Pot Roast

2 tablespoons all-purpose flour
3 pound beef chuck roast
1 medium can cream of mushroom soup
1 bay leaf
4 carrots, peeled and sliced
2 large potatoes, quartered

1) Place flour in a large microwave-safe casserole dish. Add the chuck roast, coating thoroughly on all sides. Remove excess flour. Pour the soup over meat, covering completely; add bay leaf.

2) Microwave, covered, on HIGH for 20 minutes. Turn the roast over, and spoon the soup over the roast. Microwave, covered, on MEDIUM, for 20 minutes.

3) Add the carrots and potatoes to the roast. Microwave, covered, on MEDIUM, for 20 minutes. Rotate dish and cook on MEDIUM for an additional 20 minutes or until the roast and vegetables are tender. Allow to stand for 10 minutes, covered, before removing bay leaf and serving.

Tangy Beef Stew

1 large green bell pepper, chopped
1 large onion, chopped
1 garlic clove, minced
2 tablespoons olive oil
1 pound ground beef
¼ cup tomato paste
½ cup dry sherry
1 tablespoon red wine vinegar
½ teaspoon oregano
½ teaspoon ground cumin
½ teaspoon salt
½ teaspoon pepper
⅛ teaspoon cinnamon
½ cup raisins
⅓ cup slivered almonds
1 small jar pimiento-stuffed olives, sliced

1) Combine green pepper, onion, garlic and oil. Microwave on HIGH for 5 minutes. Add ground beef and microwave on HIGH for 3 minutes, stir, and cook for an additional 2 minutes. Drain off fat.

2) Mix tomato paste, sherry and vinegar together in a bowl and stir into the meat mixture. Add oregano, cumin, salt, pepper and cinnamon. Cover and microwave on HIGH for 5 minutes.

3) Add raisins, almonds and olives and microwave, uncovered, on HIGH for 5 additional minutes.

Quick and Easy Reuben Sandwiches

¼ cup mayonnaise
1 tablespoon chili sauce
8 slices rye bread, toasted
4 slices cooked corned beef
4 slices Swiss cheese
8 ounces sauerkraut, drained

1) Mix the mayonnaise and chili sauce and spread over each slice of bread. Place the corned beef, cheese and sauerkraut on 4 slices of bread and top with the remaining bread slices.

2) Place the sandwiches on a paper towel-lined plate. Cover with a paper towel and microwave on HIGH for 1 minute, rotate the plate ½ turn and microwave an additional 1 minute, or until the cheese has melted.

English Meat Cups

Meat Cups
1 pound ground beef
1 egg, beaten
1 slice bread, crumbed
2 tablespoons catsup
¼ teaspoon salt
½ teaspoon pepper

Filling
1 small can mushroom pieces, drained
1 cup shredded Swiss cheese
¼ cup finely chopped onion

1) Combine the ingredients for the meat cups, set aside ⅓ of the mixture, and divide the remaining ⅔ into 6 muffin cups. Create a shell in each cup.

2) Combine the ingredients for the filling and place an equal portion in each cup. Use the remaining meat mixture to shape a top for each cup, and seal the edges.

3) Cook on HIGH for 10 minutes. Allow to stand for 5 minutes before serving.

Swiss Steak

1 pound round steak
2 tablespoons flour
¼ teaspoon onion powder
1 teaspoon oil
1 onion, sliced
1 cup spaghetti sauce
2 tablespoons red wine

1) Sprinkle both sides of the steak with flour, onion powder and oil.

2) Line a casserole with slices of ½ onion and place the steak on top of the onions. Microwave on HIGH for 5 minutes.

3) Top with remaining sliced onions and cover with spaghetti sauce, and red wine. Microwave, covered, on MEDIUM for 35 minutes. Allow to stand for 5 minutes.

Winter Beef Medley

¾ pound lean top round, thinly sliced against the grain
2 bay leaves
1 parsnip, finely minced
1 carrot, finely minced
¼ cup finely minced rutabagas
1 teaspoon thyme
1 tablespoon olive oil
1 tablespoon balsamic vinegar
¼ cup tomato puree
½ teaspoon minced fresh parsley
½ teaspoon freshly ground black pepper

1) Combine the top round, bay leaves, parsnip, carrot, thyme, oil, vinegar and puree. Allow to marinate, covered, in the refrigerator overnight.

2) Microwave, covered with vented plastic wrap, on HIGH for 5 minutes. Top with parsley and pepper, remove bay leaves and serve.

Classic Pot Roast

3 pounds lean pot roast
1 large can stewed tomatoes
1 package spaghetti sauce mix
1 large onion, chopped
1 cup red wine
½ cup celery, chopped
1 teaspoon seasoned salt

1) Place pot roast in a baking dish.

2) Combine remaining ingredients and pour over the pot roast. Cover with plastic wrap and microwave on MEDIUM for 60 minutes, turning meat over after 30 minutes.

English Sheperd's Pie

1 teaspoon butter
1 cup **carrots**, sliced thin
½ cup onion, chopped
1 pound ground beef, cooked and drained
1 medium can, gravy
2 cups mashed potatoes (see next page)
¼ cup Cheddar cheese, shredded

1) Mix together carrots, onion, and butter. Microwave, covered, on HIGH for 3 minutes, stir, and cook an additional 2 minutes, or until vegetables are slightly tender.

2) Mix in the meat and gravy. Microwave, covered, on HIGH for 3 minutes, stir, and cook an additional 2 minutes, or until casserole begins to bubble.

3) Arrange hot mashed potatoes around the edge of the casserole, and sprinkle with the cheese. Microwave, uncovered, on HIGH for 3 minutes, or until the cheese has melted.

Mashed Potatoes

3 potatoes
¼ cup milk
1 teaspoon butter
¼ teaspoon salt

1) Pierce the potatoes with a fork, and arrange in a circle on microwave-safe dish. Microwave, uncovered, on HIGH for 4 minutes, turn the potatoes, and cook an additional 3 minutes, or until the potatoes are tender.

2) Remove the potato pulp from the skins, and discard the skins. Mix together the potato pulp, milk, butter, and salt, mashing until smooth.

Sweet and Sour Cabbage

8 whole, fresh cabbage leaves
½ cup water
1 pound lean ground chuck
½ cup instant rice, uncooked
1 large can tomato sauce
3 tablespoons finely chopped onion
2 tablespoons brown sugar
2 tablespoons lemon juice
½ teaspoon pepper

1) Place cabbage leaves and water in a casserole, cover with plastic wrap, and microwave on HIGH for 8 minutes.

2) Combine beef, rice and onion and divide into 8 portions. Place one portion on each of the partially cooked cabbage leaves, and roll the leaf around the meat mixture. Place rolls, seam-side down, in a casserole dish.

3) Mix together the remaining ingredients and pour over the cabbage rolls. Cover with plastic wrap and microwave on HIGH for 18 minutes, rotating the dish ½ turn and basting the rolls after 9 minutes. Allow to stand, covered, for 5 minutes before serving.

Steak Teriyaki with Snow Peas

2 tablespoons soy sauce
1 tablespoon lemon juice
½ tablespoon brown sugar
½ teaspoon cornstarch
1 pound round steak, sliced across the grain into ¼-inch-thick strips
1 tablespoon sesame oil
1 garlic clove, minced
1 large onion, thinly sliced
1 teaspoon chopped fresh ginger
¼ pound snow peas
1 green pepper, cut into thin strips

1) Combine the soy sauce, lemon juice, sugar, and cornstarch. Add the beef strips and marinate for 20 minutes at room temperature.

2) Combine the oil, garlic, onion, and ginger in a pie plate and microwave on HIGH for 3 minutes.

3) Place the onion in the center of the dish, and place the meat around the outer edge of the dish, reserving the marinade. Microwave, covered, on HIGH for 3 minutes. Stir the onion and the meat together.

4) Add the reserved marinade, snow peas and pepper strips. Microwave, covered, on HIGH for 3 minutes. Serve over rice.

Burritos

1 pound ground beef
¼ cup green pepper, chopped
1 large can tomato soup
1½ tablespoon chili powder
1 tablespoon Worcestershire sauce
8 large flour tortillas
Garnish: guacamole, sour cream,
chopped tomatoes, black olives,
cilantro, hot sauce, and shredded
cheddar cheese

1) Crumble beef into a microwave-safe casserole dish. Mix in the green pepper, cover, and microwave on HIGH for 3 minutes. Stir, and cook for an additional 2 minutes or until the beef is no longer pink. Remove fat.

2) Mix in the soup, chili powder and Worcestershire. Microwave, covered, on HIGH for 5 minutes or until bubbling.

3) Wrap the entire stack of tortillas in damp paper towels. Microwave on HIGH for 1 minute.

4) Place meat and desired garnishes into individual tortillas. Fold in the sides and roll up to make burritos.

Mexican Meatballs

1 pound lean ground beef
1 slice white bread, dipped in water
and squeezed dry
1 egg, lightly beaten
¼ cup chopped cilantro
½ cup minced onion
1 large garlic clove, minced
¼ teaspoon salt
1 teaspoon chili powder
½ teaspoon ground cumin
¼ teaspoon pepper
4 ounces green chiles, diced
1 cup tomato puree

1) Combine beef, bread, egg, cilantro, ¼ cup onion, garlic, salt, ½ teaspoon chili powder, ¼ teaspoon cumin, pepper and 2 ounces chiles. Shape into bite-size meatballs.

2) Place the meatballs on a platter, cover with a paper towel, and microwave on HIGH for 6 minutes.

3) Combine tomato puree, 2 ounces chiles, ¼ cup onion, ½ teaspoon chili powder and ¼ teaspoon cumin. Cover with waxed paper and microwave on HIGH for 5 minutes, stirring once while cooking. Pour over meatballs and serve with toothpicks.

Beef and Olive Biscuits

9 ounces frozen cut green beans
¼ cup chopped onion
½ tablespoon vegetable oil
2 cups cooked beef, cut into bite-size pieces
1 cup beef gravy
¼ cup water
1 tablespoon green chiles, chopped
Olive Drop Biscuits (see next page)
¼ teaspoon paprika

1) Place the green beans, onion and oil in a casserole dish, cover, and microwave on HIGH for 4 minutes, stirring once while cooking.

2) Add the beef, gravy, water and chiles. Microwave, covered, on HIGH for 12 minutes, stirring once while cooking.

3) Place 12 dollops of dough for Olive Drop Biscuits around the edge of the dish. Top with paprika and microwave, uncovered, on HIGH (100%) for 3 minutes. Rotate the dish ½ turn and cook for an additional 3 minutes.

4) Loosely cover and allow to stand for 5 minutes before serving.

Olive Drop Biscuits

⅓ cup shortening
1¾ cups all-purpose flour
2 teaspoons baking powder
¼ teaspoon salt
1 cup milk
⅓ cup chopped pimiento-stuffed olives

1) Cut the shortening into flour, baking powder and salt until the mixture forms fine crumbs. Add milk and olives until soft dough forms.

Chuck Roast with Cloves

3 pound chuck roast, pierced with a fork
½ cup decaffinated coffee
½ cup soy sauce
1 tablespoon Worcestershire sauce
4 tablespoons red wine vinegar
8 whole cloves
1 onion, sliced
2 medium potatoes, peeled and cut into quarters
3 medium carrots, peeled and sliced

1) Combine the coffee, soy sauce, vinegar, Worcestershire and cloves in a large bowl. Place the roast in the marinade and allow to stand at room temperature for 3 hours. Turn meat every now and then.

2) Microwave, covered, on HIGH for 12 minutes. Turn the meat over and add vegetables. Microwave, covered, on MEDIUM for 1 hour. Baste 3 times while cooking. Allow to stand for 10 minutes before serving.

Beef Teriyaki

2½ pound flank steak, sliced
¾ cup soy sauce
½ cup packed brown sugar
1 clove minced garlic
2 teaspoons ground ginger
1 teaspoon pepper

1) Place slices of steak in a shallow baking dish. Blend the remaining ingredients in a bowl, mixing thoroughly.

2) Pour the marinade over the steak, cover with plastic and refrigerate at least 4 hours, preferably overnight, making sure to turn the meat over at least once while marinating.

3) Microwave on MEDIUM for 75 minutes.

Stuffed Peppers

4 green peppers
1 tablespoon water
1 pound lean ground beef
¾ cup onion, chopped
1 clove garlic, minced
½ teaspoon ground cinnamon
¼ teaspoon ground cloves
1 medium can tomato soup
1 apple, chopped
⅓ cup almonds, sliced and toasted
¼ cup raisins
1 tablespoon vinegar

1) Slice off the tops of the peppers. Chop enough pepper tops to make ⅓ cup, and set aside. Remove and discard the inner membranes and seeds from the peppers, and place the pepper shells in a microwave-safe dish.

2) Add water, and microwave, covered, on HIGH for 5 minutes, or until slightly crisp. Drain and set aside.

3) Crumble the beef into the dish, add onion, garlic, cumin, cinnamon, cloves, and chopped pepper tops. Microwave, covered, on HIGH for 3 minutes, stir, and cook for an additional 2 minutes, or until the meat is no longer pink. Remove the fat.

4) Mix in the soup, apple, almonds, raisins, and vinegar. Divide the mixture among the green and red peppers. Place in a microwave-safe dish. Microwave, covered, on HIGH for 5 minutes.

Oriental Beef

1 pound top round steak, trimmed of fat, cut into ¼-inch thick strips
¼ cup soy sauce
1 tablespoon red wine
1 tablespoon brown sugar
½ teaspoon ginger
8 ounces frozen pea pods, thawed
8 ounces canned sliced mushrooms, drained
1 cup bean sprouts, drained
¼ cup sliced green onions
4 cups cooked rice

1) Place the steak in a casserole. Mix the soy sauce, red wine, brown sugar, and ginger. Pour over steak and microwave, covered, on MEDIUM-HIGH for 6 minutes, stirring once while cooking. Drain and reserve the juice.

2) Add cornstarch and water to the reserved juice. Microwave on HIGH for 2 minutes. Stir the juices into the meat, add the pea pods, mushrooms, bean sprouts, and green onions. Microwave on MEDIUM-HIGH for 8 minutes, stirring once. Serve over cooked rice.

Hearty Hungarian Goulash

2 pounds lean beef, cubed and browned
2 tomatoes, peeled and quartered
1 large onion, minced and browned
1 cup water
¼ cup tomato puree
1 tablespoon paprika
1 tablespoon cooking oil
½ teaspoon seasoned salt
½ teaspoon coarse ground black pepper
¼ teaspoon cayenne or hot sauce

1) Place all of the ingredients in a baking dish and mix well.

2) Cover with plastic wrap and microwave on HIGH for 5 minutes. Stir, re-cover, and microwave on MEDIUM for 60 minutes, stirring twice while cooking.

Chili-Cheese Casserole

1 pound ground chuck
1 onion, sliced
½ cup chopped celery
1 large can red kidney beans, drained
1 large can whole kernel corn, drained
1 small can pitted and halved olives, drained
1 teaspoon seasoned salt
8 ounces tomato sauce
1 cup coarsely crushed corn chips
½ cup shredded Cheddar cheese
2 teaspoons chili powder
½ teaspoon pepper

1) Combine ground beef, onion, and celery in a casserole dish and microwave on HIGH for 7 minutes.

2) Mix in the remaining ingredients with the exception of the corn chips and cheese. Microwave on HIGH for 5 minutes.

3) Top with corn chips and cheese and microwave on MEDIUM-HIGH for 3 minutes. Allow to stand, covered with waxed paper, for 5 minutes before serving.

Japanese Beef with Broccoli Flowerets

2 tablespoons soy sauce
1 tablespoon lemon juice
½ tablespoon brown sugar
½ teaspoon cornstarch
1 pound round steak, sliced across the grain into ¼-inch-thick strips
1 tablespoon sesame oil
1 garlic clove, minced
1 large onion, thinly sliced
1 teaspoon chopped fresh ginger
2 cups broccoli flowerets

1) Combine the soy sauce, lemon juice, sugar, and cornstarch. Add the beef strips and marinate for 20 minutes at room temperature.

2) Combine the oil, garlic, onion, and ginger in a pie plate and microwave on HIGH for 3 minutes.

3) Place the onion in the center of the dish, and place the meat around the outer edge of the dish, reserving the marinade. Microwave, covered, on HIGH for 3 minutes. Stir the onion and the meat together.

4) Add the reserved marinade and broccoli flowerets. Microwave, covered, on HIGH for 3 minutes. Serve over rice.

Hot and Spicy Chili

1 onion, chopped
½ tablespoon vegetable oil
1 pound lean ground beef
1 large can pinto beans, with liquid
1 large can peeled plum tomatoes
with liquid, coarsely chopped
1 medium can tomato paste
1 medium can chopped green chiles,
drained
2 garlic cloves, minced
2 tablespoons chili powder
1 teaspoon ground cumin
½ teaspoon crushed hot red pepper

1) Place onion and oil in a casserole dish. Microwave on HIGH for 5 minutes, stirring once. Add beef and microwave on HIGH for an additional 2 minutes, stir, and cook for 3 more minutes.

2) Add the remaining ingredients and microwave, uncovered, for 25 minutes, stirring twice while cooking.

Spicy Hamburgers

1 pound ground beef
1 packet onion soup mix
1 teaspoon Worcestershire sauce
¼ teaspoon pepper

1) Mix all of the ingredients together, blending well. Form the mixture into patties.

2) Place in a round glass baking dish, making sure to leave space between the patties. Microwave on HIGH for 3 minutes, flip the burgers over, and cook for an additional 3 minutes.

Beef Casserole with Zucchini and Cheddar Cheese

1 cup uncooked macaroni
1 cup water
½ cup milk
1 tablespoon all-purpose flour
1 teaspoon dry mustard
2 cups sliced zucchini
1 cup shredded Cheddar cheese
2 ounces dried beef, cut up

1) Place macaroni and water in a casserole dish. Microwave, covered, on HIGH for 5 minutes. Allow to stand for 5 minutes.

2) Add milk, flour and mustard. Fold in zucchini, Cheddar cheese and dried beef. Microwave, covered, on HIGH for 8 minutes, stirring once while cooking.

Beef and Corn Casserole

1 green pepper, chopped
1 onion, chopped
1 tablespoons butter
1½ pounds ground beef
2 medium cans corn, drained
1 medium can tomato soup
1 small can mushroom slices
1 teaspoon chili powder
5 ounces noodles, cooked
½ cup shredded Cheddar cheese

1) Place the green pepper, onion and butter in a dish and microwave on HIGH for 3 minutes. Set aside.

2) Microwave beef on HIGH for 7 minutes, stirring three times while cooking. Drain.

3) Combine cooked beef, onions, peppers, corn, tomato soup, mushrooms and chili powder. Add cooked noodles. Microwave on MEDIUM-HIGH for 4 minutes, stirring once.

4) Top with shredded cheese and microwave on MEDIUM-HIGH for 1 minute.

Mushroom Round Steak

1½ pounds round steak, pounded,
cut into serving pieces
¼ cup flour
1 onion, sliced
3 tablespoons dry onion soup mix
1 tablespoon Worcestershire sauce
1 teaspoon chopped parsley plus
parsley for garnish
1 medium can cream of mushroom
soup

1) Cover the pieces of steak with flour.
Combine the remaining ingredients in a casserole. Add the pieces of steak.

2) Microwave on HIGH for 8 minutes, stir,
and microwave on MEDIUM for an additional 35 minutes. Allow to stand for 5
minutes.

Hearty Beef Chili

1½ pounds ground beef
2 large cans undrained tomatoes
2 medium cans kidney beans, undrained
1 medium can tomato paste
1 large green pepper, chopped
1½ tablespoons chili powder
½ teaspoon salt
3 teaspoons minced onion

1) Crumble beef into a large casserole dish. Mix in the remainder of the ingredients, blending well.

2) Cover with vented plastic wrap, and microwave on HIGH for 45 minutes. Let stand for 10 minutes, stir well, and serve.

Cabbage Stuffed with Beef

6 large cabbage leaves
½ cup water
1 pound ground beef
1 cup cooked rice
½ cup onion, chopped
1 large egg
1 tablespoon Worcestershire sauce
¼ teaspoon pepper
1 medium can tomato soup
1 tablespoon vinegar

1) Place the cabbage leaves in a microwave-safe dish. Add water, and microwave, covered, on HIGH for 3 minutes. Rotate the dish, and cook for an additional 3 minutes. Drain and set aside.

2) Combine the beef, rice, onion, egg, Worcestershire, pepper, and 3 tablespoons of the soup.

3) Spoon approximately ½ cup of the meat mixture onto each cabbage leaf. Fold in the sides and roll up, securing with wooden toothpicks. Mix together the remaining soup and vinegar, and spoon over the cabbage rolls.

4) Microwave, covered, on HIGH for 8 minutes, rotate dish, and cook for an additional 7 minutes, or until the meat is cooked and the cabbage is tender. Allow to stand, covered, for 5 minutes before serving.

Green Chili

2 pounds lean beef, cut into thin strips
1 tablespoon cooking oil
3 green onions, chopped
1 clove garlic, minced
8 ounces stewed tomatoes
4 ounces roasted green chili peppers, chopped
2 cups beef broth
1 cup red wine
½ teaspoon salt
½ teaspoon pepper
2 tablespoons flour
¼ cup cold water

1) Place the beef and oil in a baking dish and microwave on HIGH for 5 minutes, stirring twice while cooking.

2) Add all of the remaining ingredients with the exception of the flour. Cover with plastic wrap and microwave on MEDIUM for 50 minutes, stirring twice while cooking.

3) Combine the flour with water and stir into the chili mixture. Microwave, covered, on HIGH for 3 minutes, stirring once while cooking.

Mushroom Burgers

1½ pounds ground chuck
1 envelope dry onion soup mix
1 egg, beaten
1 tablespoon Worcestershire sauce
1 medium can cream of mushroom
soup, undiluted
⅓ cup water

1) Combine ground beef, onion soup mix, egg and Worcestershire, and shape into 6 patties. Place patties on a microwave roasting rack placed in a baking dish.

2) Cover with waxed paper and microwave on HIGH for 8 minutes. Pour off drippings.

3) Combine soup and water and pour over the patties. Cover with plastic wrap and microwave on MEDIUM-HIGH for 6 minutes.

Delicious Beef Stroganoff

2 tablespoons butter
1 onion, thinly sliced
1½ pounds beef fillet, cut across the grain into ¼-inch strips
3 tablespoons all-purpose flour
1 cup beef broth
¼ cup red wine
½ teaspoon salt
½ teaspoon pepper
¾ pound fresh mushrooms, sliced
¾ cup sour cream

1) Combine the butter and onion in a casserole dish. Microwave on HIGH for 3 minutes.

2) Coat the meat strips with the flour, and add the meat into the casserole. Cover with wax paper and microwave on HIGH for 3 minutes.

3) Add the broth, wine, salt and pepper. Microwave, covered, on HIGH for 8 minutes. Add the mushrooms, re-cover, and microwave on MEDIUM for 15 minutes.

4) Mix in the sour cream, re-cover, and microwave on MEDIUM for 3 minutes. Allow to stand, covered, for 5 minutes.

Beef Jerky
with Fresh Ginger

2 teaspoons minced fresh ginger
2 tablespoons honey
2 teaspoons sesame oil
2 tablespoons soy sauce
2 tablespoons dry white wine
2 garlic cloves, crushed
1 teaspoon cayenne pepper
1½ pounds flank steak, all fat removed, cut in thin strips

1) Combine ginger, honey, sesame oil, soy sauce, wine, garlic, and cayenne. Add steak to marinade, tossing to coat well. Marinate at room temperature, tossing occasionally, for 3 hours.

2) Remove meat from marinade and arrange half the strips, flat and close together, on a microwave bacon rack. Cover with paper towels and cook on MEDIUM-LOW 20 minutes. Rotate strips so that drier strips are in center. Cover with fresh paper towel and cook on MEDIUM-LOW 15 to 20 minutes, until meat is dry but still slightly pliable. Remove to a large wire rack and let stand overnight. Repeat with remaining strips.

Tangy Tamale Casserole

1 pound lean ground beef
1 large can whole kernel corn
1 medium can tomato sauce
1 tablespoon dry onion, minced
¼ teaspoon chili powder
¼ teaspoon salt
1 cup cheddar cheese, grated
1 small can ripe olives, sliced

Corn Bread Topping

1⅓ cup cold water
¼ teaspoon chili powder
¼ teaspoon salt
⅔ cup yellow corn meal
2 teaspoons butter

1) Combine all topping ingredients, with the exception of the butter, in a 1½ quart casserole. Microwave, covered, on HIGH for 3 minutes. Stir and cook for an additional 4 minutes or until thickened. Set aside, leaving covered.

2) Microwave ground beef on HIGH for 3 minutes in a casserole dish, stir, and cook for an additional 2 minutes.

3) Add corn, tomato sauce, chili powder, and salt to the beef. Microwave for 4 minutes, or until boiling. Add cheese and olives, stir well to mix.

4) Spread topping mixture over the casserole, cover with a paper towel, and microwave on HIGH for 4 minutes or until the corn bread is done.

5) Immediately spread butter over topping, and allow to stand for 5 to 10 minutes before serving.

Meat Loaf Ring

1½ pounds ground beef
2 eggs, beaten
½ onion, chopped
1 slice bread, crumbled
1 tablespoon Worcestershire sauce
½ teaspoon pepper
2 cups dry seasoned stuffing mix
¾ cup water
1 tablespoon butter, melted
1 small can sliced mushrooms, drained
½ onion, sliced

1) Combine the ground beef, eggs, onion, bread crumbs, Worcestershire sauce and pepper. Set aside.

2) Combine stuffing mix, water and butter. Set aside.

3) Cover the bottom of a ring mold with the mushroom and onion slices. Place ⅓ of the meat mixture on top, follow with ½ of the stuffing, repeating layers once more and finishing with a layer of meat.

4) Microwave, covered, on HIGH for 5 minutes. Reduce power to MEDIUM and cook for 10 additional minutes. Allow to stand for 5 minutes before serving.

Creamy Beef

1½ pounds sirloin steak, sliced into
thin strips and browned
1 cup sour cream
1 cup onion, sliced
1 cup mushrooms, sliced
2 teaspoons paprika
1 teaspoon Worcestershire sauce

1) Place browned beef and remaining ingredients in a baking dish. Cover with plastic
wrap and microwave on MEDIUM for 17
minutes.

Chinese Beef

¼ cup water
1½ tablespoons soy sauce
1 tablespoon dry sherry
1 tablespoon cornstarch
½ teaspoon sugar
¾ pound lean boneless beef chuck, trimmed and cut into thin strips
2 medium cloves garlic, minced
2 teaspoons fresh ginger, minced
½ teaspoon pepper
½ pound bean sprouts
⅓ cup green onion, sliced

1) Mix water, soy sauce, sherry, cornstarch, and sugar, and set aside.

2) Place meat in a microwave-safe casserole, and mix in the garlic, ginger, and pepper. Microwave, covered, on HIGH for 2 minutes. Stir, and cook for an additional 2 minutes, or until the beef is no longer pink.

3) Remove the liquid from the beef mixture and add it to the soy sauce mixture. Microwave, uncovered, on HIGH for 3 minutes, or until the sauce bubbles, thickens, and turns clear, being sure to stir once every minute.

4) Mix the sauce into the meat mixture, then add in the bean sprouts and onion. Microwave, uncovered, on HIGH for 2 minutes, stir, and cook for an additional 1 minute. Allow to stand for 1 minute before serving.

Stuffed Peppers

1½ pounds ground chuck
¼ cup finely chopped onion
⅓ cup oats, uncooked
½ teaspoon salt
¼ teaspoon pepper
1 egg, beaten
1 cup spaghetti sauce
6 green peppers, tops cut off, seeds
and membrane removed

1) Combine ground beef, onion, oats, salt, pepper, egg, and ⅓ cup spaghetti sauce. Fill the peppers with the mixture and place in a casserole dish. Pour remaining spaghetti sauce over the peppers and cover with plastic wrap.

2) Microwave on HIGH for 25 minutes. Allow to stand, covered, for 5 minutes before serving.

Chunky Chili

½ tablespoon vegetable oil
3 onions, coarsely chopped
2 garlic cloves, minced
2 pounds lean ground beef
2 green peppers, coarsely chopped
2 large cans kidney beans
1 small can tomato paste
4 cups tomatoes, chopped and peeled
8 tablespoons chili powder
1 tablespoon cumin seed
1 teaspoon dried oregano
½ teaspoon salt
½ teaspoon pepper

1) Combine the oil, onions and garlic in a large bowl. Microwave on HIGH for 5 minutes. Add in the beef, and microwave on HIGH for 12 minutes, stirring once while cooking. Drain.

2) Add the remaining ingredients. Microwave, covered, on HIGH for 10 minutes. Stir, re-cover, and microwave on MEDIUM for 40 minutes, stirring twice while cooking. Allow to stand for 5 minutes before serving.

Pot Roast
with Fennel Seeds

2 tablespoons Worcestershire sauce
3 tablespoons flour
8 ounces tomato sauce
2 garlic cloves,crushed
½ teaspoon dry mustard
½ teaspoon fennel seeds
½ tablespoon brown sugar
½ teaspoon pepper
1 4-pound boneless chuck roast, fat trimmed
4 potatoes, peeled and halved
2 carrots, peeled and chopped roughly
1 green bell pepper, chopped roughly
1 large onion, chopped roughly

1) Combine Worcestershire and flour until a paste forms. Add tomato sauce, garlic, mustard, fennel, brown sugar, pepper and salt and set aside.

2) Place the chuck roast in an oven roasting bag, and place the bag inside a casserole with a lid. Spoon the sauce over the meat, and add the potatoes, carrots, onion, and green pepper to the bag, shaking to distribute liquid evenly.

3) Cover the casserole dish and microwave on MEDIUM for 30 minutes, then turn the bag over and cook for an additional 30 minutes. If pot roast looks dry, add ¼ cup of water. Microwave on MEDIUM for 15 additional minutes, and allow to stand in bag for 25 minutes before slicing.

Steak with Green Peppers and Mushrooms

4 3-ounce beef cubed steaks
¼ teaspoon salt
¼ teaspoon pepper
4 ounces sliced mushrooms
½ cup chopped green pepper
2 tablespoons red wine

1) Place the steaks in a baking dish and sprinkle with salt and pepper. Top with mushrooms and green pepper and sprinkle with wine.

2) Cover with waxed paper and microwave on HIGH for 5 minutes. Rotate dish ½ turn and cook for an additional 5 minutes. Allow to stand for 5 minutes before serving.

Pizza Hamburger

1 pound ground beef
1 teaspoon garlic salt
½ teaspoon pepper
1 teaspoon horseradish
1 teaspoon Worcestershire sauce
1 teaspoon hot mustard
8 ounces tomato sauce
2 tablespoons dried minced onion
1 teaspoon oregano
1 cup grated Mozzarella cheese

1) Mix together the beef, salt, pepper, horse-radish, Worcestershire, and mustard. Place meat against the sides and bottom of a pie plate.

2) Pour the tomato sauce over the meat and top with onions, oregano, and cheese. Microwave on MEDIUM-HIGH for 10 minutes.

Beef with Pickled Gravy

1½ pounds beef minute steaks, scored and cut into 6 portions and flattened
2 dill pickles, cut in thirds lengthwise
6 slices bacon
1½ cups prepared brown gravy
4 tablespoons red wine
1 tablespoon Worcestershire sauce

1) Place one pickle piece and one slice of bacon on each steak. Roll up the meat and place the rolls seam side down on a roasting platter.

2) Microwave on MEDIUM for 10 minutes. Remove excess fat, place rolls in center on the outside of the dish. Combine gravy, wine and Worcestershire and pour over the meat rolls.

3) Cover with waxed paper and microwave on MEDIUM for 5 minutes.

VEAL

Veal Scallopini with Dried Tomatoes

8 dried tomatoes, minced
2 tablespoons chicken stock
1 pound veal scallopini, cut into thin strips
2 teaspoons olive oil
2 tablespoons freshly squeezed lemon juice
⅓ cup grated Mozzarella
2 tablespoons minced fresh parsley
½ pound cooked hot linguine

1) Combine the tomatoes and chicken stock in a bowl and cover with vented plastic wrap. Microwave on HIGH for 4 minutes.

2) Place the veal in a pie dish, and coat with oil and lemon juice. Cover with vented plastic wrap and microwave on HIGH for 4 minutes.

3) Combine tomatoes, mozzarella and parsley and allow to stand until the cheese melts. Toss with linguine and serve.

Veal with Mushrooms and Marsala Wine

6 veal cutlets, pounded thin and cut
into 4 pieces
⅓ cup flour
½ teaspoon salt
½ teaspoon pepper
2 tablespoons butter
1 medium can beef bouillon
½ cup mushrooms, sliced
¼ cup Marsala wine
1 teaspoon lemon juice

1) Coat pounded cutlets with flour and season
with salt and pepper. Brown cutlets in butter
in a skillet on a conventional range.

2) Place browned veal in a baking dish.

3) Combine beef bouillon, mushrooms, wine
and lemon juice and pour over cutlets. Microwave on MEDIUM for 14 minutes.

75

Veal Curry with Apples

2 tablespoons vegetable oil
1 onion, chopped
1 garlic clove, minced
1 celery rib, chopped
1 carrot, chopped
2 pounds boneless veal shoulder, cubed
2 tablespoons all-purpose flour
1 apple, peeled, cored, and cubed
2 cups chicken broth
2 tablespoons tomato paste
1 tablespoon curry powder
½ teaspoon salt
½ teaspoon pepper
½ cup plain yogurt

1) Combine the oil, onion, garlic, celery and carrot in a casserole dish. Microwave, covered, on HIGH for 4 minutes.

2) Coat the veal chunks with flour, and add the meat to the vegetables. Microwave, covered, on HIGH for 10 minutes, stirring once while cooking.

3) Add the remaining ingredients, with the exception of the yogurt. Microwave, covered, on HIGH for 8 minutes. Stir, re-cover, and microwave on MEDIUM for 50 minutes, stirring twice while cooking.

4) Add the yogurt and allow to stand, covered, for 10 minutes before serving.

Quick and Easy Veal

1½ pounds boneless loin of veal
½ cup chicken broth

1) Place the veal in a dish, add broth, and cover with plastic wrap. Microwave on HIGH for 5 minutes.

Traditional Veal Parmesan

½ cup butter
¾ cup bread crumbs
½ cup Parmesan cheese, grated
¾ teaspoon oregano
¾ teaspoon paprika
¾ teaspoon basil
¼ teaspoon salt
¼ teaspoon pepper
1¼ pounds veal cutlets, pounded thin
1 cup spaghetti sauce
1 cup mozzarella, shredded

1) Microwave butter in a shallow dish on HIGH for 1 minute or until melted.

2) Mix bread crumbs, Parmesan, oregano, paprika, basil, salt, and pepper on wax paper. Dip veal cutlets into melted butter, then coat in crumb mixture.

3) Place coated veal in a glass dish, and cover with wax paper. Microwave on MEDIUM-HIGH for 5 minutes. Top with sauce, sprinkle with mozzarella, and cover. Microwave on MEDIUM-HIGH for 3 minutes or until thoroughly heated.

Veal Scallopini California Style

1 pound veal scallopini, cut into thin pieces
2 tablespoons freshly squeezed lime juice
2 tablespoons freshly squeezed lemon juice
½ teaspoon sage
½ teaspoon honey
½ lemon, thinly sliced
½ lime, thinly sliced

1) Combine the veal, lime juice, lemon juice, sage and honey in a pie dish. Top with lemon and lime slices.

2) Cover with vented plastic wrap and microwave on HIGH for 5 minutes. Allow to stand for 2 minutes, discard the lemon and lime slices, and serve.

❖ ❖ ❖ ❖ ❖

LAMB

❖ ❖ ❖ ❖ ❖

Lamb Meatballs

1 pound lamb, ground
1 egg, beaten
¼ cup finely minced onions
2 tablespoons bread crumbs
1 clove garlic, finely minced
1 teaspoon oregano
1 tablespoon minced fresh mint
1 tablespoon lemon juice
½ cup plain low-fat yogurt
Fresh mint sprigs

1) Combine all of the ingredients with the exception of the yogurt and mint sprigs. Form into approximately 40 meatballs.

2) Place one dozen meatballs on a flat dish, cover with vented plastic wrap, and microwave on HIGH for 3 minutes. Repeat with remaining meatballs.

3) Drain the meatballs, dip in the yogurt, garnish with the mint sprigs, and serve.

Lamb Chops with Honey and Walnuts

⅓ cup honey
1 tablespoon lemon juice
¼ cup chopped walnuts
4 lamb chops

1) Combine honey, lemon juice and walnuts.

2) Place lamb chops on a roasting rack and cover tightly. Microwave on MEDIUM-HIGH, allowing 15 minutes per pound. Half-way through the cooking time, remove the lamb and drain grease. Return the lamb to the dish without the rack, coat with the honey-walnut mixture, re-cover, and complete the cooking.

Lamb Tossed with Spinach

1 pound lamb, trimmed of fat and sliced into ribbons
2 lemons, sliced
2 cloves garlic, sliced
1 teaspoon olive oil
Spinach leaves, shredded for tossing

1) Place lamb in a dish and add the lemon slices, garlic and oil. Mix well. Cover with vented plastic wrap and microwave on HIGH for 5 minutes, stirring once while cooking. Toss with the spinach and allow to stand for 5 minutes before serving.

Lamb with Apricot Glaze

4 lamb chops
1 tablespoon soy sauce
½ cup apricot jam
1 tablespoon Dijon mustard

1) Rub the lamb chops with soy sauce. Combine jam and mustard and coat the lamb with the mixture.

2) Place lamb in a baking dish, cover with plastic wrap, and microwave on HIGH for 5 minutes. Turn the chops over and spoon with sauce.

3) Re-cover, and microwave on HIGH for 5 minutes.

Lamb with Carrots, Onions and Celery

2 pounds boned lamb shoulder, cubed
1 cup water
2 teaspoons brown bouquet sauce
1 teaspoon salt
8 carrots, cut in 1-inch pieces
4 celery stalks, cut in 1-inch pieces
2 large onions, sliced
1 tablespoon Worcestershire sauce
3 tablespoons all-purpose flour
¾ cup water

1) Mix together the lamb, brown sauce, salt, and 1 cup water in a casserole dish. Cover with plastic wrap and microwave on HIGH for 5 minutes.

2) Add the carrots, celery, onions and Worcestershire sauce. Cover with plastic wrap and microwave on HIGH for 45 minutes, stirring three times while cooking.

3) Combine flour and ¾ cup water and mix into stew. Microwave on HIGH for 3 minutes and serve.

Lamb with Garlic and Mint

4 lamb shanks, cut in half across the bone
4 tablespoons minced fresh mint
4 cloves garlic, smashed and peeled

1) Place lamb in an oval dish. Top with 2 tablespoons mint and the garlic. Cover with plastic wrap and microwave on HIGH for 23 minutes.

2) Remove lamb from oven, top with remaining mint, and serve.

Leg of Lamb with Mint

1 4-pound leg of lamb, bone
removed, rolled and tied with string
1 teaspoon pepper
½ cup flour
⅓ cup dry white wine
½ cup chicken broth
2 tablespoons dried chopped mint
2 garlic cloves, minced
1 onion, minced

1) Rub the lamb with flour and pepper.

2) Combine the remaining ingredients.

3) Place the lamb in a baking dish and cover
with sauce. Microwave on MEDIUM-HIGH
for 1 hour, basting after 30 minutes.

4) Allow to stand for 10 minutes before
carving.

Lamb Stew

2 pounds lamb, cubed
2 tablespoons flour
1 medium can tomato soup
2 cups potatoes, diced
1 cup dry white wine
**2 tablespoons cooking oil, browned
in a skillet**
½ teaspoon basil
¼ teaspoon pepper
1 clove garlic, minced
1 head cabbage, cut in wedges

1) Dust lamb with flour. In a baking dish, combine all of the ingredients with the exception of the cabbage.

2) Cover with plastic wrap, and microwave on HIGH for 5 minutes. Reduce to MEDIUM, and microwave for 15 minutes.

3) Add cabbage, re-cover, and microwave on MEDIUM for 15 minutes.

Greek-Style Lamb

**4-pound leg of lamb, boned, rolled
and tied with string
½ cup Dijon mustard
2 tablespoons olive oil
2 tablespoons ground ginger
1 tablespoon soy sauce
2 teaspoons thyme
1 garlic clove, pressed**

1) Combine all of the marinade ingredients, brush over the lamb, and refrigerate for 5 hours.

2) Microwave on MEDIUM-HIGH for 1 hour.

3) Allow to stand for 10 minutes before carving.

❖　❖　❖

PORK AND HAM

❖　❖　❖

Old-Fashioned Polish Sausage

1 pound Polish sausage, cooked, slashed every 2 inches
1 onion, sliced
12 ounces beer
1 tablespoon hot mustard
¼ teaspoon pepper

1) Combine all of the ingredients in a casserole, and microwave, covered, on HIGH for 10 minutes.

Hot Links with Peppers and Basil

2 pounds hot Italian sausage links, cut into 2-inch lengths
1 large red bell pepper, stemmed, seeded and sliced
1 large green bell pepper, stemmed, seeded and sliced
1 large onion, peeled and cubed
¼ cup fresh basil leaves
¼ cup tomato sauce

1) Place sausage in a dish and cover with a paper towel. Microwave on HIGH for 10 minutes, stirring twice while cooking. Drain.

2) Add the remaining ingredients, mixing well. Cover tightly with plastic wrap and microwave on HIGH for 7 minutes.

Sausage with Fennel

2 pounds hot Italian sausage links, cut into 2-inch lengths
¾ cup bulb fennel, cut into 2-inch chunks
1 large red bell pepper, stemmed, seeded and sliced
1 large onion, peeled and cubed
¼ cup tomato sauce
1 teaspoon fennel seeds

1) Place sausage in a dish and cover with a paper towel. Microwave on HIGH for 10 minutes, stirring twice while cooking. Drain.

2) Add the remaining ingredients, mixing well. Cover tightly with plastic wrap and microwave on HIGH for 7 minutes.

Sausage and Mushroom Casserole

1 pound pork sausage
1 onion, chopped
1 green pepper, chopped
½ cup chopped celery
1 cup cooked rice
1 medium can cream of mushroom soup, undiluted
1 medium can cream of chicken soup, undiluted
1 small jar pimiento, chopped and drained
1 small can mushrooms, drained
1 cup shredded Cheddar cheese

1) Place the sausage in a baking dish. Microwave on HIGH for 6 minutes, stirring once while cooking.

2) Add the onion, green pepper and celery. Microwave on HIGH for 5 minutes and drain.

3) Add the rice, soups, pimento and mushrooms to the sausage mixture. Cover with waxed paper and microwave on HIGH for 6 minutes.

4) Top with Cheddar cheese and microwave on HIGH, covered, for 2 minutes.

Hawaiian Pork

1 12-ounce pork tenderloin
1 medium can pineapple chunks in juice, drained, 2 tablespoons juice reserved
2 tablespoons chili sauce
2 tablespoons dry white wine
1 tablespoon soy sauce
2 green onions, thinly sliced
1 clove garlic, finely chopped
1 slice ginger root, smashed
3 tablespoons honey
1 teaspoon cornstarch
1 tablespoon cold water
Cooked rice

1) Place pork tenderloin in baking dish. Combine pineapple chunks, reserved juice, chili sauce, wine, soy sauce, green onions, garlic and ginger root, and pour over pork. Cover and refrigerate for 3 hours, turning once while marinating.

2) Remove pork and place on a microwave rack in a baking dish and reserve marinade. Brush pork with honey, cover with waxed paper, and microwave on MEDIUM for 3 minutes. Rotate dish ¼ turn and continue to cook for 3 additional minutes.

3) Turn the pork over, brush with honey, re-cover, and microwave for 9 minutes, rotating ¼ turn twice while cooking.

4) Combine cornstarch and water and mix into marinade. Re-cover once again and microwave on HIGH for 3 minutes. Cut pork diagonally into ¼-inch slices and serve with pineapple sauce over rice.

Pork Spareribs with Glaze

3 pounds pork spareribs cut into serving pieces
1 onion, quartered
½ green pepper, quartered
2 garlic cloves
1 teaspoon Worcestershire sauce
½ cup catsup
⅓ cup dark brown sugar
¼ cup dark molasses
¼ cup lemon juice
1 teaspoon dry mustard

1) Combine all of the ingredients with the exception of the spareribs.

2) Place half of the ribs in a large baking dish and microwave, covered, on MEDIUM-HIGH for 8 minutes. Drain, and repeat with remaining spareribs.

3) Baste half of the ribs with sauce and microwave, covered, on MEDIUM-HIGH for 15 minutes. Repeat with the remaining ribs and serve.

Pork Chops with Rice and Cheese

6 pork chops
2 onions, sliced
2 tablespoons Parmesan cheese
1 cup uncooked instant rice
1 cup spaghetti sauce
2 tablespoons water
1 cup grated Mozzarella cheese

1) Place pork chops in a casserole dish. Top with onion slices and microwave, covered, on HIGH for 7 minutes.

2) Combine remaining ingredients and pour over the chops. Microwave, covered, on HIGH for 7 minutes. Reduce power to MEDIUM and cook for an additional 15 minutes.

Pork Chops with Barbecue Sauce

4 loin pork chops
3 green onions, chopped
1 cup barbecue sauce
2 tablespoons orange juice
2 tablespoons brown sugar
½ teaspoon salt
½ teaspoon pepper

1) Place pork chops in a roasting platter. Combine remaining ingredients and pour over chops. Cover with plastic wrap and cook on MEDIUM for 25 minutes, rotating the dish once while cooking.

Pork Chops
with Tomatoes and Rice

⅓ cup chopped onion
⅓ cup chopped green pepper
⅓ cup chopped celery
1 large can tomatoes
1 envelope instant tomato soup mix
1½ cups quick-cooking long grain rice, uncooked
1 teaspoon salt
1 teaspoon pepper
6 loin pork chops

1) Combine onion, green pepper and celery in a casserole dish. Cover with waxed paper and microwave on HIGH for 2 minutes.

2) Add tomatoes, soup mix, rice, salt and pepper. Place on top of the onion mixture, and place the chops on top of that.

3) Cover with plastic wrap and microwave on HIGH for 5 minutes. Rotate dish ¼ turn, and microwave on MEDIUM for 18 minutes. Allow to stand, covered, for 5 minutes before serving.

Oriental Pork

1 tablespoon vegetable oil
6 scallions, cut into 1-inch pieces
1 garlic clove, minced
1 medium can unsweetened
pineapple chunks, drained, liquid
reserved
2 cups cooked pork, diced
2 tablespoons vinegar
2 tablespoons brown sugar
1 tablespoon cornstarch

1) Combine oil, scallions and garlic and microwave on HIGH for 1 minute.

2) Add the pineapple chunks and pork to the scallions and garlic.

3) Combine the reserved pineapple juice, vinegar, brown sugar and cornstarch. Add into the pork mixture and microwave on HIGH for 3 minutes, stirring twice while cooking.

Pork Roast with Herbs

4-pound pork boneless top loin roast
1 clove garlic, cut into halves
3 teaspoons dried marjoram leaves
3 teaspoons dried sage leaves
1 teaspoon pepper
Pork Gravy (see below)

1) Rub the pork roast with garlic.

2) Mix marjoram, sage and pepper together and sprinkle over pork roast. Place roast fat side down on a microwave rack in a baking dish. Cover with waxed paper and microwave on MEDIUM for 10 minutes.

3) Rotate dish ½ turn and cook for 12 additional minutes. Turn roast fat side up, re-cover, and microwave for 30 minutes, rotating the dish ½ turn twice while cooking. Cover with aluminum foil and allow to stand for 15 minutes.

Pork Gravy

¼ cup drippings from baking dish
¼ cup all-purpose flour
1¾ cups water

1) Combine ingredients into a casserole dish and microwave on HIGH for 5 minutes, stirring once while cooking. Serve on the side.

Garlic Pork Chops with Sauerkraut

1 tablespoon butter
1 large onion, peeled, thinly sliced
4 loin pork chops
2 pounds sauerkraut, drained and rinsed
1 tablespoon caraway seeds
4 cloves garlic, smashed and peeled
1 cup sour cream
1 tablespoon paprika

1) Place butter in a dish and microwave on HIGH for 2 minutes. Add onions, and microwave on HIGH for 2 minutes.

2) Place pork chops on top of the onions, meaty side in the center of the dish. Cover chops with sauerkraut and top with caraway seeds. Add garlic and cover with plastic wrap. Microwave on HIGH for 15 minutes.

3) Add sour cream and paprika. Re-cover and microwave on HIGH for 2 minutes.

Pork with Sweet and Sour Sauce

1½ pounds pork tenderloin, cubed
1 tablespoon cornstarch
1 tablespoon soy sauce
2 tablespoons brown sugar
3 tablespoons vinegar
¼ teaspoon ginger
1 small can pineapple chunks and juice
1 large onion, sliced and separated
1 large green pepper, cut into strips

1) Combine pork and cornstarch in a casserole dish. Add remaining ingredients, with the exception of the green pepper.

2) Microwave, covered, on MEDIUM-HIGH for 15 minutes. Add green pepper, re-cover, and cook for an additional 15 minutes. Allow to stand for 5 minutes before serving.

Korean Pork

2 tablespoons sesame seeds, toasted
3 cloves garlic, finely minced
½ teaspoon minced fresh ginger
2 scallions, very finely minced
1 teaspoon soy sauce
1 teaspoon honey
1 teaspoon freshly squeezed lemon juice
1 pound lean top round, sliced against the grain into thin ribbons

1) Combine the sesame seeds, garlic, ginger, scallions, soy sauce, honey and lemon juice. Add beef, toss, and allow to marinate for 2 hours.

2) Place beef in a casserole, cover with vented plastic wrap and microwave on HIGH for 7 minutes, stirring twice while cooking. Allow to stand for 3 minutes before serving.

Pork Chops Stuffed with Herbs and Wine

1 onion, finely chopped
⅓ cup celery, finely chopped
1 tablespoon butter
1 cup dried bread crumbs
2 tablespoons parsley, chopped
¼ teaspoon celery seed
¼ teaspoon sage
4 thick pork chops, sliced to form a pocket
2 tablespoons flour
¼ cup dry white wine

1) Combine onion, celery and butter and microwave on HIGH for 4 minutes.

2) Add the bread crumbs, parsley, celery seed and sage. Fill the pockets of the pork chops with the stuffing, securing the openings with wooden toothpicks.

3) Place the stuffed pork chops in a roasting platter, with the meatiest portions facing the outside of the dish. Top with flour, chicken broth and wine, cover with plastic wrap, and microwave on MEDIUM for 35 minutes, rotating the dish once while cooking.

Pork Chops
with Apple Slices

4 thick pork chops, sliced to form a pocket
1 cup stuffing mix
⅓ cup hot water
1 tablespoon butter, melted
¼ teaspoon salt
¼ teaspoon pepper
2 tablespoons red wine
8 apple slices
¼ cup brown sugar

1) Combine stuffing mix, hot water, butter, salt and pepper. Fill the pocket of each chop with the stuffing.

2) Place the stuffed chops in a baking dish, with the thick portion of the chop facing the outside of the dish. Brush with wine and top with 2 apple slices.

3) Cover with waxed paper and microwave on MEDIUM for 12 minutes. Rotate dish, sprinkle apples with brown sugar, re-cover, and cook for an additional 18 minutes.

Classic Barbecue
Spare Ribs

3 pound rack of pork ribs
2 cups hot tap water
1 lemon, sliced
1 large onion, sliced
2½ cups barbecue sauce

1) Place ribs, bone side up, in a large microwave-safe dish. Add water, and cover tightly with vented plastic wrap.

2) Microwave on MEDIUM for 20 minutes, rotate the dish ½ turn, and cook for an additional 20 minutes, or until tender.

3) Turn ribs over and place lemon and onion on top of the ribs. Microwave on MEDIUM for 20 minutes, rotate the dish ½ turn, and cook for an additional 20 minutes.

4) Drain the liquid from the ribs and pour the barbecue sauce over the top of the ribs. Microwave on MEDIUM for 15 minutes and serve.

Chinese Pork with Broccoli Flowerets

1 tablespoon vegetable oil
6 scallions, thinly sliced
3 tablespoons water
1 tablespoon sherry
2 teaspoons soy sauce
1 teaspoon cornstarch
2 cups cooked pork, cubed
4 cups broccoli flowerets

1) Combine the oil and scallions, and microwave on HIGH for 1 minute.

2) Combine the water, sherry, soy sauce and cornstarch, and add to the scallions. Mix in the pork cubes, coating well.

3) Microwave on HIGH for 2 minutes, stirring once while cooking. Add the broccoli, and microwave, covered, on HIGH for 3 minutes, stirring once while cooking.

Chinese Sweet and Sour Pork

1½ pounds pork, cubed
2 tablespoons soy sauce
1½ tablespoons minced onion
1 medium can pineapple chunks
1 cup water
¼ cup brown sugar
¼ cup cider vinegar
2 tablespoons cornstarch
¼ teaspoon salt
1 medium can water chestnuts, drained and sliced
1 large green pepper, sliced
1 large tomato, cubed

1) Place pork, soy sauce, and onion in a casserole. Drain pineapple juice and set pineapple chunks aside. Add pineapple juice to pork, stirring well, and cover. Microwave on MEDIUM for 15 minutes, stir, and cook for an additional 15 minutes.

2) Mix together the water, vinegar, brown sugar, cornstarch and salt. Add the mixture, pineapple chunks, and water chestnuts to the meat. Microwave, covered, on MEDIUM-HIGH, for 8 minutes. Stir and add green pepper and cook for an additional 10 minutes, or until the mixture is thick and clear.

3) Add the tomato and let stand, covered, for 10 to 15 minutes before serving.

Chinese Pork with Vegetables

1½ cups cubed cooked pork
1½ cups pork gravy
1 cup sliced celery
1 large can Chinese vegetables, rinsed and drained
1 small can sliced mushrooms, drained
1 small jar sliced pimiento, drained
1 teaspoon soy sauce

1) Combine all ingredients in a casserole dish. Microwave, covered, on HIGH for 12 minutes, stirring once while cooking.

Easy-To-Make Bratwurst

1 pound bratwurst, uncooked
1 can of beer
1 large can sauerkraut

1) Combine bratwurst and beer in a microwave-safe casserole dish, cover, and microwave on HIGH for 5 minutes.

2) Reduce to MEDIUM-HIGH and microwave for an additional 20 minutes, stirring twice.

3) Microwave sauerkraut on HIGH for 2 minutes. Spread sauerkraut on serving platter and spoon bratwurst mixture on top.

Mexican Chorizo with Eggs

1 pound pork chorizo sausage
½ cup green onion, chopped
½ cup green chili peppers, chopped
1 large fresh tomato, chopped
¼ teaspoon chili powder
1 tablespoon butter
8 eggs, beaten
4 tablespoons milk
¼ teaspoon salt
¼ teaspoon pepper
1 large can refried beans
6 large flour tortillas
¾ cup cheddar cheese, grated

1) Microwave chorizo on HIGH in a casserole for 5 minutes, and set aside.

2) Combine onion, chili peppers, tomato, and chili powder in a microwave-safe bowl. Microwave on HIGH for 4 minutes, and set aside.

3) Melt butter in a glass pie dish. Add eggs and milk, blending well. Microwave on HIGH for 5 minutes, or until eggs are moist but not dry, stirring twice. Add salt and pepper to taste.

4) Drain chorizo, if necessary, and add the two mixtures, stirring gently. Cover to keep warm.

5) Place the beans in a 1 quart casserole and microwave on HIGH for 1½ minutes. Stir and cook for an additional 1½ minutes.

6) Microwave the tortillas on a paper towel for 1 minute. Place a hot tortilla on a plate, spread with a thin layer of beans, cover with the chorizo mixture, top with cheese, and microwave on HIGH for 1 minute or until cheese begins to melt. Repeat with each tortilla.

Pork Chops
with Orange Sauce

4 pork loin chops, about ½-inch thick
1 onion, thinly sliced
Grated peel of 1 orange
Juice of 1 orange
¼ cup red wine
1 clove garlic, finely chopped
1 tablespoon brown sugar
¼ teaspoon ground cloves
1 orange, thinly sliced
1 teaspoon cornstarch
1 tablespoon cold water

1) Arrange the pork chops with the narrow ends toward the center of the baking dish. Place onion slices on top of the pork.

2) Combine the orange peel, orange juice, wine, garlic, brown sugar and cloves. Pour the mixture over the pork and microwave, covered, on MEDIUM for 5 minutes. Rotate the dish ¼ turn and cook for an additional 5 minutes.

3) Place the orange slices on top of the pork, rotate the dish ½ turn, re-cover, and cook for an additional 15 minutes, rotating the dish ¼ turn twice while cooking. Remove pork chops and cover with aluminum foil.

4) Combine 1 cup of juices from the baking dish with cornstarch and water. Microwave, covered, on HIGH for 2 minutes. Spoon sauce over pork chops and serve.

Pineapple Pork Steaks

4 pork blade steaks, about ½-inch thick
1 teaspoon instant beef bouillon
1 medium can pineapple chunks in juice, drained
2 cups soft bread cubes
½ cup chopped celery
¼ cup chopped onion
2 tablespoons margarine, melted
¼ teaspoon ground cinnamon
¼ teaspoon ground sage

1) Arrange pork steaks on a microwave rack in a baking dish with meaty edges towards the edge.

2) Microwave, covered, on MEDIUM for 15 minutes, rotating baking dish ¼ turn twice while cooking. Drain and sprinkle the pork with bouillon.

3) Combine the remaining ingredients and spoon over the pork steak. Microwave, covered on MEDIUM for 20 minutes, rotating baking dish ¼ turn every 5 minutes. Allow to stand 5 minutes before serving.

Ham and Raisins

½ cup raisins
½ cup red currant jelly
½ cup hot water
Peel of 1 orange, grated
½ cup orange juice
1 tablespoon brown sugar
1 teaspoon Dijon mustard
¼ teaspoon ground allspice
1 cooked ham steak

1) Combine raisins, jelly, water, orange peel and orange juice. Microwave on HIGH for 3 minutes, stirring once while cooking.

2) Combine brown sugar, mustard and allspice. Stir into orange mixture and microwave on HIGH for 1 minute, stirring once while cooking.

3) Microwave ham steak, covered, on MEDIUM-HIGH, for 7 minutes. Pour sauce over ham and serve.

Ham with Honey and Bananas

3 pounds ham, sliced
1 jar whole cloves
2 tablespoons hot mustard
½ cup honey
¼ cup white wine
¼ teaspoon cinnamon
4 bananas, cut lengthwise in strips
1 can apricot halves, drained

1) Score the edges of the ham. Place cloves into the fat edges and spread the hot mustard over the surface.

2) Place ham on a microwave-safe dish. Combine honey, wine, and cinnamon, and baste the ham with the sauce.

3) Microwave, covered with wax paper, on HIGH for 6 minutes, basting twice. Brush bananas and apricots with sauce, and place on top of the slices of ham.

4) Pour the remainder of the sauce over the ham and microwave, uncovered, on HIGH for 4 minutes.

Hawaiian Ham and Beans

1 cup ½-inch pieces fully cooked ham
1 large can butter beans, drained
1 can large baked beans in molasses sauce
1 medium can lima beans, drained
¼ cup chopped onion
1 teaspoon Dijon mustard
1 medium can pineapple chunks in juice, drained

1) Combine all of the ingredients with the exception of the pineapple in a casserole dish. Microwave, covered, on HIGH for 12 minutes, stirring once while cooking. Top with pineapple chunks and serve.

Hawaiian Kabobs

1 medium can pineapple chunks in juice
½ cup dark corn syrup
2 tablespoons corn oil
1½ tablespoons cider vinegar
⅛ teaspoon ground cloves
½ pound ham steak, cubed
2 large oranges, cut into 12 pieces
1 teaspoon cornstarch

1) Drain pineapple chunks, reserving the juice. Combine juice, syrup, oil, vinegar and cloves in a shallow dish.

2) Pierce the ham cubes with a fork, and add the ham, pineapple chunks, and orange slices to the marinade. Cover and refrigerator over night.

3) Alternate ham, pineapple, and oranges on six wooden skewers and place on a microwave-safe plate.

4) Mix the cornstarch into the marinade, blending until smooth. Microwave marinade on HIGH 1 minute, stir, and cook an additional 2 minutes.

5) Baste the ham kabobs with the hot marinade, and microwave on HIGH for 3 minutes. Baste, turn, and microwave on HIGH for 3 minutes.

Smoked Ham with Creamy Corn Sauce

1 medium can cream-style corn
2 tablespoons chopped green pepper
½ tablespoon butter
1 teaspoon instant minced onion
1 egg, beaten
½ cup diced fully cooked smoked ham
½ cup shredded Cheddar cheese
½ cup crushed crackers

1) Combine corn, green pepper, butter and onion in a casserole dish. Cover and microwave on HIGH for 3 minutes.

2) Add egg, ham, cheese, and ¼ cup cracker crumbs. Microwave, covered, on MEDIUM-HIGH for 2 minutes. Stir, top with remaining cracker crumbs, re-cover, and cook for an additional 5 minutes.

Ham and Asparagus Rolls

1 pound fresh asparagus
2 tablespoons water
8 slices boiled ham
1 medium can cream of celery soup
½ cup plain yogurt
¼ cup milk
2 tablespoons fresh parsley, chopped
1 teaspoon hot mustard

1) Arrange asparagus with tips toward center in a microwave-safe baking dish. Add water, and cover with vented plastic wrap.

2) Microwave on HIGH for 2 minutes, rotate dish, and cook for an additional 2 minutes, or until asparagus is tender. Drain well.

3) Roll the slices of ham around the cooked asparagus, securing with wooden toothpicks. Place the rolls in the baking dish.

4) Stir soup until smooth, and mix in the yogurt, milk, parsley, and hot mustard until thoroughly blended. Pour the mixture over the ham rolls.

5) Cover with vented plastic wrap, and microwave on MEDIUM for 15 minutes or until thoroughly heated. Allow to stand, covered, for 5 minutes before serving. Serve with or over rice, if desired.

Ham and Cheese Sandwiches

2 cups sliced mushrooms
1 clove garlic, finely chopped
1 small onion, sliced
½ tablespoon butter
4 thin slices cooked smoked ham
4 slices rye bread, toasted
4 thin tomato slices
4 slices Cheddar cheese

1) Place mushrooms, garlic, onion, and butter in a casserole dish. Microwave, covered, on HIGH for 5 minutes, stirring once while cooking.

2) Place 1 ham slice on each slice of toast, and top with equal amounts of the mushroom mixture. Place 1 tomato slice and 1 slice of cheese on top of the mushroom mixture.

3) Arrange sandwiches in a circle on a paper towel-lined plate. Microwave on HIGH for 2 minutes, rotating the plate ½ turn after 1 minute.

VARIETY MEATS

Mom's Liver and Onions

1 large onion, thinly sliced
1 tablespoon vegetable oil
1 pound chicken livers, rinsed,
drained and cut into chunks
½ teaspoon garlic powder
½ teaspoon salt
½ teaspoon pepper

1) Combine onion slices and oil, and microwave on HIGH for 4 minutes. Remove onions and set aside.

2) Season liver with garlic powder, salt and pepper and microwave, covered, on MEDIUM for 7 minutes, stirring once while cooking.

3) Re-heat the onion on HIGH for 30 seconds. Combine with liver and serve.

Rabbit with Creamy Mustard Sauce

**2 pounds frozen rabbit, cut into serving pieces
2 cups milk
1 cup cream
1 cup Dijon mustard
3 tablespoons fresh lemon juice
½ teaspoon salt
½ teaspoon freshly ground black pepper**

1) Place rabbit, boney side up, in a dish. Preheat a conventional broiler.

2) Combine remaining ingredients, and pour over the rabbit. Cover with plastic wrap and microwave on LOW for 8 minutes, uncover, turn rabbit over, and cook for an additional 7 minutes.

3) Re-cover and microwave on HIGH for 18 minutes. Remove rabbit and place in a broiling pan. Brush with the cooking liquid and broil for 3 minutes, until lightly browned.

Smoked Tongue with Garlic-Beer Sauce

4 pounds smoked tongue, trimmed
¾ cup dark beer
1 cup water
1 tablespoon brown sugar
2 cloves garlic, smashed and peeled

1) Place tongue in a dish. Combine remaining ingredients and pour over tongue. Cover with plastic wrap, and microwave on HIGH for 10 minutes.

2) Uncover, and turn tongue over. Re-cover and cook for an additional 10 minutes. Remove from oven, uncover, and allow to cool.